THE ULTIMATE CHICAGO BEARS BOOK FOR KIDS AND TEENS

160+ Fun, Surprising, And Educational Stories And Trivia Quizzes About Players And History

John Stevenson

First published 2024

ISBN 9798344469331

Contents

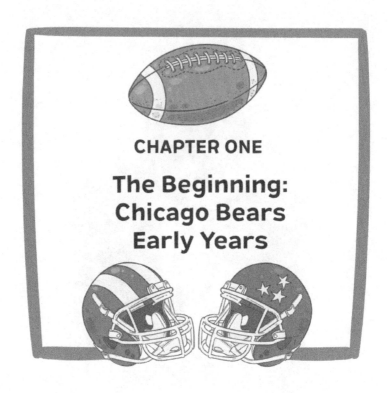

CHAPTER ONE

The Beginning: Chicago Bears Early Years

The Chicago Bears are one of the oldest and most famous teams in the NFL. Their story goes back to 1920 when a man named George Halas started the team.

But, believe it or not, the Bears weren't called the Chicago Bears at first. They were known as the Decatur Staleys for the first two years because they played in Decatur, Illinois. The Decatur Staleys were part of the A. E. Staley food starch company's team. It was common for early pro football teams to be a part of companies back then.

In 1920, the company hired George Halas to run the team. Halas had big plans and moved the team to Chicago in 1921. They became the Chicago Staleys for that season, but it wasn't long before they got the name we know today.

In 1922, the team changed their name to the Chicago Bears. The name "Bears" was chosen because it was bigger and tougher than the city's baseball team, the Chicago Cubs. Cubs are baby bears, and football players are bigger and stronger than baseball players!

When the Bears moved to Chicago, they played their games at Wrigley Field. It was the same stadium where the Cubs played. The Bears stayed there until 1971 when they moved to Soldier Field, their home ever since.

From the very beginning, the Bears were a successful team. They were even the first team ever to buy a player from another team. One of their biggest rivals was the Chicago Cardinals, the oldest team in the NFL at the time. Today, those Cardinals are known as the Arizona Cardinals.

The Bears had a lot of great moments, especially in the 1940s. They made it to four straight NFL championship games and won three of them.

But the 1950s were tough, and they only made one playoff appearance. In 1963, they finally broke a long 17-year streak without a championship by beating the New York Giants 14-10.

A lot of the Bears' success came from their founder, George "Papa Bear" Halas. He wasn't just the owner. He was also a player, coach, and general manager. Halas did it all for the Bears for over 60 years. When he retired as a coach in 1967, he had more coaching victories than anyone else, with 324 wins. That record stood for 27 years.

One of the Bears' biggest moments came in 1985 when they won their first Super Bowl. They defeated the New England Patriots in Super Bowl XX. They had an amazing defense with stars like Mike Singletary and Richard Dent. Even though they continued winning games in the late 1980s, they never made it back to the Super Bowl during that time.

In 2006, the Bears won their second NFC Championship. They were led by quarterback Rex Grossman and head coach Lovie Smith. The Bears went on to Super Bowl XLI, but they were defeated by the Indianapolis Colts.

Today, the Chicago Bears are one of the two original NFL teams that still exist, along with the Arizona Cardinals. They've won nine NFL championships, the most in league history.

The Bears have worked hard from their early days as the Decatur Staleys to becoming Super Bowl champions. They remain one of the greatest teams in NFL history.

CHAPTER ONE QUIZ

1. What year were the Chicago Bears founded?

a. 1920

b. 1923

c. 1929

d. 1934

2. What was the Chicago Bears' original name?

a. Decatur Jackets

b. Decatur Birds

c. Decatur Staleys

d. Decatur Shirts

3. What is the name of the founder of the Chicago Bears?

a. Joe Carr

b. Jimmy Conzelman

c. Guy Chamberlin

d. George Halas

4. Which team did the Chicago Bears defeat in 1985 to win their first Super Bowl?

a. Brooklyn Dodgers

b. New England Patriots

c. Green Bay Packers

d. Chicago Cardinals

5. In which year did the Bears win their second NFC Championship?

a. 2000

b. 2006

c. 2010

d. 2015

6. Who was the Bears' quarterback during their Super Bowl XLI loss to the Indianapolis Colts?

a. Rex Grossman

b. Justin Fields

c. Mitchell Trubisky

d. Jay Cutler

Quiz Answers

1. 1920 **2.** Decatur Staleys **3.** George Halas **4.** New England Patriots **5.** 2006 **6.** Rex Grossman

CHAPTER TWO

Famous Rivalries

As the Chicago Bears became one of the most popular NFL teams, many major rivals look to defeat the Bears every time they meet.

Here are three of the Bears' fiercest rivals, whose intense matchups have produced some of the most exciting and memorable moments in NFL history.

Green Bay Packers

The rivalry between the Green Bay Packers and the Chicago Bears is one of the fiercest and oldest in the NFL. Both teams play in the NFC North, which makes them natural rivals. Every time the Packers and the Bears play, the games are filled with excitement and intense competition!

It all started back in 1921 when the Packers and Staleys faced off for the first time. In that game, the Packers lost 0-20, and the rivalry was born.

But things really heated up on November 23, 1924. The Bears' player Frank Hanny and the Packers' player Tillie Voss started throwing punches on the field. They both got kicked out of the game, making it the first-ever NFL ejection. From that day on, the rivalry only got more intense.

One of the most unforgettable games between the Bears and Packers happened on November 17, 1963. It was a chilly day at Wrigley Field. Both teams were fired up, ready to battle for first place in the Western Conference. The Bears and Packers each had an impressive 8-1 record, so everyone knew it was going to be a tough game.

The Packers had won the last two championships. But, the Bears were ready to prove they were stronger. From the moment the game started, the Bears' defense was unstoppable. They crushed the Packers, making it nearly impossible for them to do much of anything. The Bears won the game 26-7.

That win also set the stage for something even bigger. The Bears went on to finish the season with a victory in the NFL Championship game. It was their 8th NFL Championship!

Each time these teams meet, it feels like a big showdown. Both teams try to knock the other out of playoff spots or ruin their chances of winning a title. With every game, the rivalry gets stronger!

Minnesota Vikings

Did you know the Bears have another big rival besides the Packers? There's another team that gets the Bears all fired up - the Minnesota Vikings! Since they're in the same division, they play at least twice a season. Those games are super important, especially if it's close to playoff time.

The rivalry started way back when the Vikings joined the league in 1961. They had their first game on September 17, 1961. That day, the Vikings shocked everyone by winning 37–13 in Minnesota. That was just the beginning of a fierce rivalry.

Over the years, these teams have had some really intense moments. One memorable game took place on October 9, 2022. The Vikings beat the Bears 29-22, but it was a nail-biter.

The Vikings were ahead 21–10 by halftime, but the Bears didn't give up. They came roaring back, scoring 19 points and even taking the lead 22–21 with just over 9 minutes left. The Bears might not have won, but their comeback effort showed their heart, and the fans loved it.

Lately, the Vikings have had the edge, but every time these two teams meet, it's a thriller. Fans know it's going to be an exciting game when the Bears and Vikings face off!

Detroit Lions

Since the Bears and Lions are in the same division, they meet twice every season. This rivalry started way back in 1930. That was when the Portsmouth Spartans, who later became the Detroit Lions, joined the NFL.

In the early years, the Bears were one of the best teams in the league and dominated the rivalry. One of the most famous games happened in 1932. That was when the Bears played the Lions (then still the Spartans) in the first-ever NFL playoff game.

The weather was so bad that they had to play indoors at Chicago Stadium. The Bears won 9-0, claiming the league championship. They showed everyone how strong they were in those early days.

By the 1950s, the Lions were getting better and becoming one of the top teams in the league. But by the 1960s and 1970s, the Bears were back in control of the rivalry. Both teams struggled during the early 2000s, as they went through rebuilding years.

Recently, the Bears-Lions rivalry has heated up again. One unforgettable game took place in 2019, on Thanksgiving Day. The Bears won 24-20 in an exciting showdown. The game kept fans on the edge of their seats, with both teams playing hard till the very end.

Whether it's a Thanksgiving Day matchup or an important game late in the season, you know it's going to be a battle whenever the Bears and Lions face off.

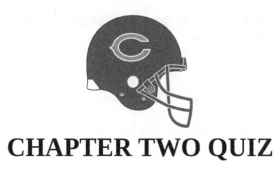

CHAPTER TWO QUIZ

1. What started the rivalry between the Green Bay Packers and the Chicago Bears?

a. Both teams compete in the NFC North division

b. The Packers defeated the Bears at the Super Bowl

c. There is a rivalry between Wisconsin and Illinois

d. The Bears traded their best players to the Packers

2. What year did the Bears and Packers play against each other for the first time?

a. 1920

b. 1921

c. 1926

d. 1930

3. What year did the Bears and Vikings play against each other for the first time?

a. 1955

b. 1961

c. 1964

d. 1968

4. What was the Detroit Lions' original name?

a. Portsmouth Spartans

b. Portsmouth Lions

c. Portsmouth Rangers

d. Portsmouth Commanders

Quiz Answers

1. Both teams compete in the NFC North division **2.** 1920 **3.** 1961 **4.** Portsmouth Spartans

CHAPTER THREE

Legendary Players

The Chicago Bears have some of the greatest players to play in the NFL. Since the beginning of the NFL, the Bears have produced the most Hall of Famers.

These famous Bears players have shown what it means to play for the Chicago Bears, whether they are winning the Super Bowl or scoring a point.

WALTER PAYTON

1X SUPER BOWL CHAMPION (XX)

1X NFL MVP

5X FIRST-TEAM ALL-PRO

9X PRO BOWL

BORN
July 25, 1953
Columbia, Mississippi, U.S.

POSITION
Running back

NFL DRAFT
1975 / round: 1 / Pick: 4

Walter Payton was one of the greatest players in Chicago Bears and NFL history. He was the heart and soul of the Bears for 13 seasons, playing from 1975 to 1987. He didn't start playing football until his junior year of high school. His older brother, Eddie, was the team's star, and Walter didn't want to compete with him. But after Eddie graduated, the coach encouraged Walter to try out.

Even though he wasn't especially big, Walter's speed and strength made him one of the best players on the team. His high school football career started with a bang. He ran for a 65-yard touchdown on his very first carry! From that moment on, everything seemed to fall into place.

Walter quickly became known as one of the best running back prospects in Mississippi. He had offers from many big colleges. But, he chose to attend Jackson State University, where his brother Eddie played football. At Jackson State University, Walter's personality quickly won over his teammates.

"Man, you run sweet as sugar," his teammate said after watching Walter dance through defenders in practice. "We ought to call you 'Sweetness.'"

The nickname stuck, though Walter's running style was anything but sweet to defenders. One opposing coach remarked, "That boy runs like he's angry at the ground." He broke several school records and was selected for the All-American Team.

In 1975, the Chicago Bears drafted Walter Payton in the first round with the fourth overall pick. But joining the Bears wasn't easy. The team was struggling, losing a lot of games, and didn't have much going for them in the mid-70s. Walter's debut game in a Bears uniform didn't go as planned. He didn't gain any yards in eight carries. His first game was a harsh reality check.

"Zero yards?" he muttered in the locker room, staring at the stat sheet. "This ain't happening again." Walter was determined to improve. That offseason, he worked tirelessly. Every day, he ran up and down a steep hill in the scorching Mississippi heat. The hard work paid off.

In his second season, Walter found his rhythm, rushing for 1,390 yards and scoring 13 touchdowns. He was voted to the Pro Bowl and was named the game's MVP. By his third season, he rushed for 1,852 yards and 16 touchdowns, leading the league in scoring.

One of the most unforgettable games of Walter's career happened in 1977. That year, he rushed for an NFL record of 275 yards in a single game! It was against the Bears' division rival, the Minnesota Vikings.

When Mike Ditka became the head coach of the Bears in 1985, everything clicked for Walter. That season, he rushed for over 1,500 yards. Teams tried everything to stop him, but he would always do damage on the field.

Walter played two more seasons after the Bears' famous Super Bowl win in 1985. He retired after the 1987 season. By the time he hung up his cleats, he had rushed for an incredible 16,726 yards. It broke the record for the most rushing yards by any player in NFL history.

His number, 34, was retired by the Bears, and he was inducted into the Pro Football Hall of Fame in 1993.

MIKE SINGLETARY

1X SUPER BOWL CHAMPION (XX)

2X NFL DEFENSIVE PLAYER OF THE YEAR

7X FIRST-TEAM ALL-PRO

10X PRO BOWL

BORN
October 9, 1958
Houston, Texas, U.S.

POSITION
Linebacker

NFL DRAFT
1981 / round: 2 /
Pick: 38

Mike "Samurai Mike" Singletary was one of the toughest and hardest-hitting players in NFL history. He was part of the Bears' famous "Monsters of the Midway" defense in the mid-1980s. Mike wasn't the biggest linebacker. But, he was so intense that he was once penalized for yelling at himself.

"Who are you yelling at?" the confused referee asked.

"MYSELF!" he roared. "I'M BETTER THAN THAT!"

The referee threw the flag, later explaining, "I've never seen anyone that intense about their own performance."

Before joining the Bears, Mike was a star linebacker at Baylor University in Texas. One day, he was pushing himself through another intense workout in the gym when his coach walked in.

"Mike, you're already the strongest player on the team," the coach said. "Why are you still here at midnight?"

Mike, dripping with sweat, barely looked up. "Because somewhere out there, someone's trying to be better than me. And I won't let that happen."

His intensity was legendary even in college. That was how Mike became Baylor's first three-time All-American. He was named the Southwest Conference Player of the Decade for the 1980s. It was a huge honor that spanned the entire league, not just his school.

In 1981, Mike was drafted by the Chicago Bears and quickly made his mark. By his seventh game as a rookie, he became a starter. In a game against the Kansas City Chiefs, Mike recorded an incredible 10 tackles and forced a fumble. It was only his third start! Everyone was amazed, and it was no surprise when he made the all-rookie team.

In 1985, Mike led the Bears to an outstanding 15-1 season. The "46" defense, created by coach Buddy Ryan, allowed Mike to go unblocked on almost every play. That year, he racked up

109 solo tackles, 3 sacks, and an interception. He won the NFL Defensive Player of the Year award and helped lead the Bears to a Super Bowl final.

It was the night before the big game. While head coach Mike Ditka was talking to the offense, Mike was in charge of motivating the defense.

The meeting started quietly. But soon, Mike started giving a fiery motivational speech. He started talking about warriors and battle. Suddenly, chairs were flying and guys were flipping tables. He got everyone fired up to play their best.

Mike Singletary retired in 1992 after an incredible 12 seasons with the Bears. He started 172 games, the second most in team history.

On August 1, 1998, Mike was inducted into the Pro Football Hall of Fame. Mike's size never stopped him from becoming the Bears' top tackler in eleven straight seasons. He is forever remembered as one of the greatest linebackers of all time.

BRIAN URLACHER

1X NFL DEFENSIVE PLAYER OF THE YEAR

NFL 2000S ALL-DECADE TEAM

4X FIRST-TEAM ALL-PRO

8X PRO BOWL

BORN
May 25, 1978
Pasco, Washington, U.S.

POSITION
Linebacker

NFL DRAFT
2000 / round: 1 /
Pick: 9

Brian Urlacher is one of the greatest defensive players in Chicago Bears history. He was a first-round draft pick in 2000 who quickly became the NFL Defensive Rookie of the Year. He went on to win Defensive Player of the Year. He led the Bears to an NFC Championship. Brian played all of his career with the Bears and retired as one of the best middle linebackers ever.

Brian was always goofing around off the field like a big kid. Before a game, he was up to his usual antics in the Bears' locker room. He crept up behind linebacker Lance Briggs with a handful of grass.

"Brian, don't you dare..." Briggs warned, but he was too late. Brian stuffed the grass into his helmet, cackling like a kid on a playground.

"Come on, Lance!" Brian grinned. "It's for good luck!"

His humor made everyone love him. Despite being a star player, he was always humble and kind. But when the team took the field for warmups, a different Brian emerged. He turned into a fierce, unstoppable force. He chased down quarterbacks and running backs, slamming his big, tough body into them.

As a linebacker, Brian had everything a team needed. He was a leader and a commanding presence on the field. Standing 6-4 and weighing 260 pounds, he struck fear into the hearts of opposing players. Running backs dreaded going up against him. They knew he could deliver a huge hit whenever the Bears needed it.

One of his most legendary performances came in 2006. It was during a game against the Arizona Cardinals. The Bears were losing by 20 points. But, Brian helped lead an incredible comeback. He made a career-best 25 tackles and forced a fumble that was returned for a touchdown.

Brian also led the Bears to Super Bowl XLI as their middle linebacker. Even though the Bears lost to the Indianapolis Colts 29-17, Brian had an impressive game. He recorded seven tackles, four assists, and a pass defensed.

In May 2013, Brian Urlacher retired after 13 amazing seasons with the Bears. In 2018, he was honored with a spot in the Pro Football Hall of Fame.

DAN HAMPTON

1X NFL SUPER BOWL CHAMPION (XX)

NFL 1980S ALL-DECADE TEAM

1X FIRST-TEAM ALL-PRO

4X PRO BOWL

BORN
September 19, 1957
Oklahoma City,
Oklahoma, U.S.

POSITION
Defensive tackle

NFL DRAFT
1974 / round: 1 /
Pick: 4

33

Dan Hampton grew up on a farm near Cabot, Arkansas, in the 1960s. His family worked hard. They baled hay, fed animals, and grew a huge vegetable garden.

"Son," his father said, wiping sweat from his brow, "hard work builds character. Remember that."

When Dan was a young child, he had a terrible accident. He fell 45 feet from an elm tree and broke both of his legs. He was stuck in a wheelchair for six months and couldn't play sports for years.

By the time he was in eighth grade, he decided to join the junior high football team. But after just a few practices, Dan told his mom it hurt too much. So, he quit and joined the school band instead.

But football wasn't done with Dan yet. A coach from Jacksonville High School saw Dan's size and knew he had potential. He begged Dan to give football another try. Finally, Dan agreed.

When he joined the team in 11th grade, they put him at right offensive tackle. Pretty soon, Dan was turning heads with his strength. He was so powerful, he could block multiple players at once. He did it by running straight ahead with his arms spread wide!

"Holy smokes!" his coach shouted. "Did you guys see that? That's not blocking, that's bulldozing!"

Dan's talent earned him a scholarship to the University of Arkansas. But at first, he wasn't a standout player. NFL scouts didn't think much of him because he weighed only 240 pounds and wasn't very fast.

Dan didn't let that discourage him, though. He worked harder than ever, training for three hours a day, six days a week. By the time scouts returned for his senior year, they were shocked.

"Hampton's different this year," a scout said to his colleague. "He's transformed himself."

Dan had gained 20 pounds of muscle, and his speed had improved. He was named an All-American. He won the Southwestern Conference's Defensive Player of the Year and Lineman of the Year awards.

The Chicago Bears couldn't pass up on his talent, so they picked him fourth overall in the 1979 NFL Draft. As a rookie, Dan made an instant impact. He recorded 70 tackles, two fumble recoveries, and two sacks. Thanks to his hard work on the defensive line, the Bears won ten games and made it to the playoffs.

Dan was nicknamed "Danimal" for his ferocious style of play. He battled through ten knee surgeries and other injuries throughout his career.

In 1985, he helped the Bears win Super Bowl XX. Dan retired in 1990 after twelve seasons with the Bears. He was inducted into the Pro Football Hall of Fame in 2002.

DEVIN HESTER

NFL 2000S ALL-DECADE TEAM

NFL 2010S ALL-DECADE TEAM

3X FIRST-TEAM ALL-PRO

4X PRO BOWL

BORN
November 4, 1982
Riviera Beach, Florida, U.S.

POSITION
Wide receiver / Return specialist

NFL DRAFT
2006 / round: 2 /
Pick: 57

Devin Hester is one of the most exciting and unique players in NFL history. He played eight seasons for the Bears, from 2006 to 2013. During that time, he became one of the most dangerous return specialists the league had ever seen. Devin led the NFL three times in punt return touchdowns.

When Devin was still a sophomore, a scout spotted him playing. The University of Miami was facing North Carolina State.

But, the scout's eyes were fixed on one player in particular. He watched as the speedy player caught the opening kickoff 5 yards deep in the end zone.

"Oh my God," he whispered, gripping his notepad tighter.

In a blink, Devin was gone, racing down the field for a touchdown! The scout knew right then that the Bears needed to sign this kid.

The Chicago Bears selected Devin in the second round of the 2006 NFL draft. They originally drafted him as a cornerback. But from the moment he stepped on the field, he made his mark on special teams. In his very first NFL game, Devin returned a punt for an 84-yard touchdown.

By the end of his rookie season, he had set an NFL record with five kick return touchdowns. He earned the nickname "Anytime." Everyone believed that he could score a touchdown anytime he touched the ball.

One of Devin's biggest moments came in Super Bowl XLI against the Indianapolis Colts. As he stood deep to receive the opening kickoff, Colts kicker Adam Vinatieri turned to his special teams coach.

"Should we kick it deep?" Vinatieri asked.

Before the coach could answer, the ball was in the air. Seconds later, Devin was making history with a 92-yard return for a touchdown. He became the first player ever to open a Super Bowl with a kickoff return touchdown. After that, the Colts avoided kicking the ball to him for the rest of the game.

In 2007, Devin continued to set records. He returned four kickoffs and two punts for touchdowns. He created an NFL record that year for six combined kick returns for touchdowns.

Teams were so afraid of him that they began kicking the ball away from him. It often led to bad kicks and giving the Bears' offense great field position.

"I want you to kick the ball into Lake Michigan and make sure it sinks to the bottom!" shouted Rod Marinelli, head coach of the Detroit Lions, his face red with exasperation. "Just don't let Hester get the ball!"

In his final season with the Bears, Devin broke the team record for most kickoff return yards in a game with 249. By the time his Bears career ended in 2013, he had averaged 27.7 kickoff return yards and 14.2 punt return yards.

He joined the Atlanta Falcons in 2014 and eventually retired from the NFL in 2017.

On February 8, 2024, Devin Hester made history once again. He became the first return specialist ever to be inducted into the Pro Football Hall of Fame.

STEVE MCMICHAEL

1X SUPER BOWL CHAMPION (XX)

2X FIRST-TEAM ALL-PRO

2X PRO BOWL

BORN
October 17, 1957
Houston, Texas, U.S.

POSITION
Defensive tackle

NFL DRAFT
1980 / round: 3 /
Pick: 73

Steve "Mongo" McMichael was a defensive tackle who played football with the energy of a rockstar and the fierceness of a wild animal. He would slam into quarterbacks and leave his opponents stunned.

Off the field, Steve was larger than life. He was intimidating, proud of being part of an elite defense, and always full of personality. He was known for calling every guy he spoke to "brother."

Before becoming a Bear, Steve was an All-American and the defensive MVP at the University of Texas at Austin. He was drafted by the New England Patriots in 1980 but only played in six games before they released him.

As fate would have it, the Chicago Bears were watching. One of their defensive linemen had gone down with an injury. Defensive coordinator Buddy Ryan decided to make an important call.

"Get me that McMichael kid," Ryan barked into the phone. "I've got a feeling about him."

Steve quickly made an impact as a starting defensive tackle. Little did the Bears know, they had just signed an "ironman" who would make their defense unstoppable.

At 6-feet-2 and 270 pounds, Steve was big, tough, and hard to beat. He led the team in sacks and tackles, stopping other teams cold with no mercy. During film sessions, he would study opponents with the same intensity he brought to the field.

"Look at this quarterback here," he'd say, pointing at the screen. "He's got a tell. Every time he's gonna pass, he taps his left foot. Brother, that's all I need to know."

His powerful defense helped the Bears win six division titles and the Super Bowl XX in 1986. From 1982 to 1991, the Bears allowed fewer points, rushing yards, and total yards than any other team in the NFL. Steve helped set records for the

Bears, including the fewest yards allowed and the most sacks in 1984.

One of Steve's most unforgettable moments came during a 1991 game against the New York Jets. The Bears were losing 13–6 with only 1:54 left, and it looked like there was no hope.

But Steve wasn't about to give up. He forced a fumble, recovered the ball at the Jets' 36-yard line, and gave the Bears a chance.

Quarterback Jim Harbaugh threw a game-tying touchdown with 18 seconds left. Then, the Bears won in overtime! Without Steve's determination, that victory wouldn't have been possible.

Steve's last year with the Bears was in 1993. He played one final season with the Green Bay Packers in 1994 before retiring. On August 3, 2024, Steve was inducted into the Pro Football Hall of Fame.

RICHARD DENT

2X SUPER BOWL CHAMPION (XX, XXIX)

1X SUPER BOWL MVP

1X FIRST-TEAM ALL-PRO

4X PRO BOWL

BORN
December 13, 1960
Atlanta, Georgia, U.S.

POSITION
Defensive end

NFL DRAFT
1983 / round: 8 /
Pick: 203

Richard Dent is known as the best pass rusher in Chicago Bears history. He's a Hall of Famer and one of the greatest players ever to wear the Bears' navy blue and orange jersey.

But when the Bears first drafted him, no one expected him to become a football legend. Richard was just a skinny kid from Tennessee State. Although NFL scouts liked his speed, they were worried about his small size. They didn't think he could handle the tough, physical play in the NFL.

Because of these concerns, team after team passed on Richard during the 1983 NFL Draft. He kept waiting and waiting, but his name wasn't called. Finally, in the eighth round, the Chicago Bears picked him as the 203rd overall player.

From the moment he arrived at training camp, Richard felt like he had something to prove. Even though he was chosen in the eighth round, he believed he was a star player deep down. He was a fantastic pass rusher in college. But, being drafted so late made him feel disappointed. He became determined to show everyone they were wrong about him.

At first, some of his new Bears teammates weren't sure what to make of him. Dan Hampton, another player on the team, thought Richard seemed lazy during his first week of practice.

"Hey Hampton, what do you think of Dent?" asked Buddy Ryan, the Bears' defensive coordinator.

"Eh, I don't know. He seems kind of lazy," Hampton replied. "I don't think he'll give it his all."

But Buddy Ryan wasn't ready to give up on Richard. "Don't judge him too quickly. He's smart. Dent never makes a bad move on the field." Sure enough, Richard started to impress everyone after another week of training camp.

Richard exceeded all expectations right from the start. He had a special gift for knowing when opponents were trying to block or trap him. He quickly showed that he was something special.

In his rookie season in 1983, he played in every game and started three of them. That year, he set a team record with 17.5 sacks, the most by any defender in the NFC. Over the next few seasons, he only got better. By his second and third years, he had 34.5 sacks.

The Bears' famous 46 defense, created by Buddy Ryan, let Richard use his incredible speed. He could get past offensive tackles and take down quarterbacks. He became a key part of the Bears' legendary defense of the 1980s.

One of Richard's greatest moments came in Super Bowl XX when the Bears crushed the New England Patriots 46-10. Richard was unstoppable, recording 1.5 sacks, forcing two fumbles, and even blocking a pass. His performance was so impressive that he was named the game's MVP, a rare honor for a defensive player.

After the 1993 season, Richard left the Bears to play for the San Francisco 49ers. But, he came back to Chicago for one last season in 1995.

He retired after the 1997 season with an incredible 137.5 sacks and eight interceptions in his career. In 2011, Richard Dent was inducted into the Pro Football Hall of Fame.

RICHARD MARVIN BUTKUS

NFL 1960S ALL-DECADE TEAM

NFL 1970S ALL-DECADE TEAM

5X FIRST-TEAM ALL-PRO

8X PRO BOWL

BORN
December 9, 1942
Chicago, Illinois, U.S.

POSITION
Linebacker

NFL DRAFT
1965 / round: 1 /
Pick: 3

Richard "Dick" Butkus was the meanest and fiercest middle linebacker to ever put on a helmet. He wasn't just tough. He was downright scary! After being a two-time All-American at the University of Illinois, he became the heart of the Chicago Bears' defense.

Dick struck fear into NFL offenses. He was known for being a ferocious tackler, growling and grunting like a grizzly bear when he lined up to play. If you were on the other team, you knew you were in for a rough day when Dick Butkus was on the field.

Dick was born into a big, hard-working family on the South Side of Chicago. By the time he was in fifth grade, he knew he wanted to become a professional football player. He chose his high school, summer jobs, and friends carefully. Everything he did was to help him become a pro player one day.

That dream came true when Dick was drafted into the NFL as the third overall pick in 1965. He was the best linebacker out of Illinois, and Chicago Bears coach George Halas knew they had to draft him. Halas and Butkus shared more than just football. They were both from Chicago. They were first-generation Americans with a fierce love for the game.

"Son," Halas said, extending his hand, "welcome home."

"Coach," Dick replied, his grip firm, "I've been a Bear my whole life. Now I get to wear the uniform."

Dick made an impact right away as a rookie. At 6 feet 3 inches tall and 245 pounds, he was huge. But, he was also quick. He could tackle players from one sideline to the other. He covered tight ends and running backs on passing plays. He had everything a great linebacker needed: speed, strength, instincts, and leadership.

For eight straight years, Dick led the Monsters of the Midway. Even though the Bears kept performing poorly, he earned his place among the best players in the league. He was like a heat-seeking missile, hitting anyone in his path.

Other linebackers looked up to him as the gold standard, the player they all wanted to be like. He made his mark as one of the best middle linebackers of all time.

Sadly, Dick's career was cut short by knee injuries, and he only played for nine seasons. But in that time, he earned a spot in eight Pro Bowls and made All-Pro eight times. He recorded 1,020 tackles, 22 interceptions, and 27 fumble recoveries.

His opponents feared him, his teammates admired him, and he became a legend in football.

In 1979, Dick Butkus was inducted into the Pro Football Hall of Fame. He wasn't just a Monster of the Midway. He was like Godzilla, unstoppable and larger than life.

CHAPTER THREE QUIZ

1. Which year was Walter Payton drafted by the Chicago Bears?

a. 1970

b. 1971

c. 1975

d. 1977

2. Why did Walter Payton wait until his older brother graduated from high school before he started playing football?

a. He was too small-sized to play football

b. He had disciplinary issues in school

c. He thought that he was too slow

d. He did not want to compete with his older brother

3. What position did Walter Payton play?

a. Quarterback

b. Running back

c. Center

d. Wide receiver

4. How many times was Walter Payton selected for the Pro Bowl?

a. 6

b. 8

c. 9

d. 11

5. What was Walter Payton's nickname?

a. Sweetness

b. Minister of Defense

c. Chuckles

d. Hard Knocks

6. Which college did Mike Singletary play for?

a. University of Tennessee

b. Baylor University

c. University of Alabama

d. University of Mississippi

7. What prestigious award did Mike Singletary win in college?

a. Heisman Memorial Trophy

b. Maxwell Award

c. Southwest Conference Player of the Decade for the 1980s

d. Chuck Bednarik Award

8. How many seasons did Mike Singletary play for the Chicago Bears?

a. 5 seasons

b. 6 seasons

c. 8 seasons

d. 12 seasons

9. How many games did Mike Singletary start during his career with the Chicago Bears?

a. 104 games

b. 159 games

c. 172 games

d. 222 games

10. What award did Brian Urlacher win in his rookie season?

a. NFL Defensive Rookie of the Year

b. NFL Offensive Rookie of the Year

c. NFL Most Valuable Player

d. NFL Comeback Player of the Year

11. Which year was Brian Urlacher drafted by the Chicago Bears?

a. 1999

b. 2000

c. 2005

d. 2007

12. What is Brian Urlacher famous for?

a. Player who played the most NFL games

b. Being one of the best middle linebackers ever in NFL history

c. Fastest player in the NFL history

d. Player with the most NFL MVP awards

13. How many times was Brian Urlacher selected for the First-Team All-Pro?

a. 4

b. 8

c. 10

d. 11

14. What year was Brian Urlacher inducted into the Pro Football Hall of Fame?

a. 2017

b. 2018

c. 2020

d. 2022

15. What year did Brian Urlacher retire from football?

a. 2010

b. 2011

c. 2012

d. 2013

16. How many seasons did Dan Hampton play for the Chicago Bears?

a. 5 seasons

b. 7 seasons

c. 10 seasons

d. 12 seasons

17. What position did Dan Hampton play?

a. Defensive tackle

b. Running back

c. Tight end

d. Wide receiver

18. Which college did Dan Hampton play for?

a. Ohio State

b. Clemson University

c. University of Michigan

d. University of Arkansas

19. What year did Dan Hampton win the NFL Defensive MVP award?

a. 1980

b. 1982

c. 1983

d. 1985

20. What was Dan Hampton's nickname?

a. Danimal

b. The Diesel

c. A-Train

d. The Kid

21. What special achievement did Devin Hester accomplish in Super Bowl XLI against the Indianapolis Colts?

a. He became the first Bear to score a touchdown in a Super Bowl

b. He became the first rookie to score a touchdown in a Super Bowl

c. He became the first player to score three touchdowns in a Super Bowl

d. He became the first player ever to open a Super Bowl with a kickoff return touchdown

22. What NFL record did Devin Hester create in 2007?

a. 83-yard punt return touchdown

b. 6 combined kick returns for touchdowns

c. 108-yard missed field goal return

d. 94-yard kickoff return

23. What position was Devin Hester drafted to play?

a. Quarterback

b. Running back

c. Tight end

d. Cornerback

24. How many seasons did Devin Hester play for the Chicago Bears?

a. 5 seasons

b. 8 seasons

c. 10 seasons

d. 12 seasons

25. Which team did Devin Hester join in 2014 after departing from the Bears?

a. Jacksonville Jaguars

b. Cincinnati Bengals

c. Atlanta Falcons

d. Miami Dolphins

26. Which NFL team did Steve McMichael play for before he joined the Chicago Bears?

a. Cincinnati Bengals

b. Pittsburgh Steelers

c. Cleveland Browns

d. New England Patriots

27. What was Steve McMichael's nickname?

a. Mongo

b. The Eagle

c. The Jailer

d. Magician

28. How many times was Steve McMichael selected for the Pro Bowl?

a. 1

b. 2

c. 3

d. 4

29. Which college did Steve McMichael play for?

a. Ohio State

b. Mississippi State University

c. University of Texas at Austin

60

d. University of Southern California

30. Which year was Steve McMichael inducted into Pro Football Hall of Fame?

a. 2017

b. 2020

c. 2022

d. 2024

31. Why didn't NFL scouts want Richard Dent, even though he was an outstanding college player?

a. He did not pass his exams

b. He was considered too small for the NFL

c. He had disciplinary problems

d. He was not good at throwing and did not have a strong arm

32. Which round was Richard Dent selected in the 1983 NFL Draft?

a. 3rd round

b. 5th round

c. 6th round

d. 8th round

33. How many sacks did Richard Dent record in Super Bowl XX?

a. 1.5 sacks

b. 2 sacks

c. 3 sacks

d. 4 sacks

34. How many sacks did Richard Dent record in his whole career?

a. 100 sacks

b. 120 sacks

c. 137.5 sacks

d. 143 sacks

35. What year did the Chicago Bears draft Dick Butkus?

a. 1960

b. 1963

c. 1965

d. 1972

36. Which year was Dick Butkus elected to the Pro Football Hall of Fame?

a. 1971

b. 1974

c. 1979

d. 1987

37. How many tackles did Dick Butkus get during his NFL career?

a. 1,020 tackles

b. 1,370 tackles

c. 1,490 tackles

d. 1,530 tackles

Quiz Answers

1. 1975 **2.** He did not want to compete with his older brother **3.** Running back **4.** 9 times **5.** Sweetness **6.** Baylor University **7.** Southwest Conference Player of the Decade for the 1980s **8.** 12 seasons **9.** 172 games **10.** NFL Defensive Rookie of the Year **11.** 2000 **12.** Being one of the best middle linebackers ever in NFL history **13.** 4 times **14.** 2018 **15.** 2013 **16.** 12 seasons **17.** Defensive tackle **18.** University of Arkansas **19.** 1982 **20.** Danimal **21.** He became the first player ever to open a Super Bowl with a kickoff return touchdown **22.** 6 combined kick returns for touchdowns **23.** Cornerback **24.** 8 seasons **25.** Atlanta Falcons **26.** New England Patriots **27.** Mongo **28.** 2 times **29.** University of Texas at Austin **30.** 2024 **31.** He was considered too small for the NFL **32.** 8th round **33.** 1.5 sacks **34.** 137.5 sacks **35.** 1965 **36.** 1979 **37.** 1,020 tackles

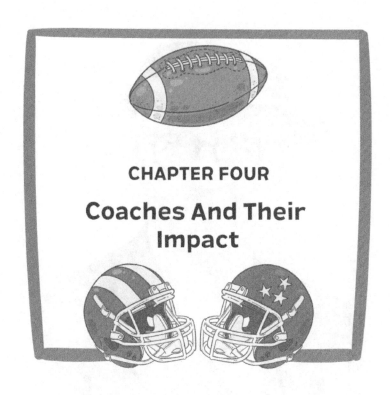

CHAPTER FOUR

Coaches And Their Impact

Behind every great NFL team is a visionary head coach who inspires players and creates a winning culture. During the Bears' long history, many legendary head coaches have guided the team through Super Bowl finals and challenges from the sidelines.

George Halas is known as the father of the Chicago Bears, and his influence on the team is legendary. People often called him "Papa Bear," and for good reason! He was the Bears' coach from 1920 to 1967 and led the team to six NFL championships.

Halas wasn't just a coach, though. He was also known as "Mr. Everything." In the early days, he did just about every job for the Bears. He was the coach, played as a wide receiver and defensive end, and even sold tickets! He was so good that he was named to the NFL's All-Pro team in the 1920s. On top of all that, he ran the entire team as its owner until he passed away in 1983.

One of the reasons Halas was such a great coach was his creativity. He came up with new ideas for the T-formation offense. It changed how teams played football during his time. He was also really good at adapting his coaching style to fit his players' strengths.

Off the field, Halas was a pioneer. He made the Bears the first team to hold daily practices. This is normal today but groundbreaking back then. He was also the first coach to study the films of other teams to determine their weaknesses. Halas was also a strict coach who demanded respect and discipline from his players.

By the time he retired, Halas had 318 wins as a head coach, making him the winningest coach in NFL history for many years. His incredible career truly helped shape the Bears and the NFL.

Another important coach for the Bears was Mike Ditka. He was the head coach for 10 seasons, from 1982 to 1992, and he made a huge impact by leading the Bears to a Super Bowl win. Before becoming head coach, Mike Ditka was a star player for the Bears. He played tight end and was selected by Chicago as the fifth overall pick in the 1961 NFL draft. Ditka became one of the top players in Bears history. After retiring as a player,

Ditka began his coaching career as an assistant coach with the Dallas Cowboys. But even then, he had his eye on coming back to Chicago.

While working with the Cowboys, Ditka sent a letter to George Halas, his former head coach. He asked for a chance to return to the Bears as the head coach. George Halas decided to give him that chance, making Ditka head coach in 1982. Right after taking the job, Ditka called a team meeting. He made a bold promise to his players. He would take them to the Super Bowl within three seasons if they worked hard and followed his plan.

Ditka was known for his tough love style and didn't put up with nonsense. But he was determined to make the Bears champions. By his third season in 1984, Ditka led the Bears to the NFC Championship Game. Even though they lost to the San Francisco 49ers, everyone could see that Ditka was turning the Bears into a powerhouse team.

The biggest moment for Ditka came on January 26, 1986, when he led the Bears to Super Bowl XX. By this time, the Bears had the best defense in the entire NFL. With quarterback Jim McMahon leading the offense, they dominated the game. The Bears crushed their opponents and won the Super Bowl.

"Iron Mike" ended his time as Bears head coach with two NFL Coach of the Year awards and a Super Bowl championship. He also had 106 total wins, the second-highest in franchise history. He will always be remembered as the coach who brought the Bears their first Super Bowl victory.

CHAPTER FOUR QUIZ

1. What was George Halas' nickname?

a. Mr. Bear

b. Papa George

c. King Bear

d. Papa Bear

2. How many NFL Championships did the Bears win with George Halas as their coach?

a. 2 times

b. 4 times

c. 6 times

d. 8 times

3. How many games did George Halas win as a head coach?

a. 267 wins

b. 299 wins

c. 318 wins

d. 357 wins

4. Which year did Mike Ditka join the Bears as head coach?

a. 1976

b. 1982

c. 1988

d. 1993

5. How many Super Bowls did Mike Ditka win with the Bears?

a. 1

b. 2

c. 3

d. 4

6. What position did Mike Ditka play when he was a player for the Bears?

a. Running back

b. Quarterback

c. Tight end

d. Wide receiver

7. How many seasons did Mike Ditka coach the Bears?

a. 5 seasons

b. 7 seasons

c. 8 seasons

d. 10 seasons

CHAPTER FIVE

Memorable Moments in Bears' History

The Chicago Bears have had some amazing moments that fans will never forget.

From winning the Super Bowl in 1985 to special moments like Gale Sayers' six-touchdown game in 1965, here are five exciting and unforgettable moments in Bears history.

SUPER BOWL XX VICTORY (1986)

The Chicago Bears were having the best football season anyone could remember in 1985. They had a defense so powerful that it seemed like they were unstoppable. Their coach, Mike Ditka, was tough and no-nonsense. Defensive coordinator, Buddy Ryan, had designed a defense called the "46 Defense" that confused and crushed almost every offense they faced.

As the Bears won game after game, everyone in Chicago started to believe that this team could do something special. They finished the regular season with a 15-1 record. That meant they only lost one game the whole season!

When the playoffs started, the Bears didn't slow down. They shut out the New York Giants and the Los Angeles Rams. The "46 Defense" did not let either team score a single point.

On January 26, 1986, the Bears faced the New England Patriots in New Orleans. The team was led by quarterback Jim McMahon, linebacker Mike Singletary, defensive end Richard Dent, and running back Walter Payton.

As the teams warmed up on the field, Jim McMahon gathered the offense in a huddle.

"Listen up, boys," he said, his voice intense. "We've come too far to let this slip away. Let's show them what the Bears are made of!"

From the opening kickoff, it was clear this would be a battle. The Patriots quickly took a lead. They kicked a field goal and took a quick 3-0 lead. But the Bears didn't panic. They had a plan, and they knew their defense could shut down the Patriots.

By halftime, the Bears were winning 23-3, and it felt like the game was already over. The Patriots couldn't move the ball at all. They even lost 19 yards in the first half. The Bears continued to pile on points in the second half, extending the lead to 44-3.

By the end of the game, the scoreboard read 46-10. The Bears had crushed the Patriots, and their victory was one of the biggest blowouts in Super Bowl history. As navy blue, orange, and white confetti rained down on the field, Richard Dent was named Super Bowl MVP.

The win brought a renewed sense of pride and excitement to Bears fans. They had waited so long and faced many disappointments in the playoffs. It was a victory they would never forget!

THE BEARS' FIRST NFL CHAMPIONSHIP (1933)

In 1933, something big happened for the Chicago Bears. They won their first NFL Championship! But this wasn't just any championship. Back then, football was different. The NFL was still a young league, and there wasn't even a Super Bowl yet.

That year, the league decided to do something different. They were going to hold the first-ever official NFL Championship Game. The Bears were ready to make history.

The Bears were already a well-known team by 1933, thanks to the legendary George Halas. The team had done really well that season, winning 10 games and only losing two. They had earned the right to play in the first-ever NFL Championship Game.

The Bears faced the New York Giants on December 17, 1933. The game was held at Wrigley Field in Chicago. It was the same famous stadium where the Chicago Cubs baseball team played.

It was a cold day, with 26,000 fans in the stands. Everyone was bundled up and eager to see who would win the first-ever NFL title.

1933 was also a special year for the NFL. This was the first season when teams were allowed to use the forward pass more often. Before that, teams mostly ran the ball. But, now they could throw it! George Halas was quick to take advantage of this new rule. Now, the Bears had become even more dangerous on offense.

The Bears and the Giants battled back and forth in a tough, hard-hitting game. The Bears took the lead early, but the Giants weren't about to give up. The Giants fought back and even took the lead in the second quarter. The game was close throughout, with both teams trading touchdowns and big plays.

The Bears were down 21-16 in the fourth quarter, and time was running out. It seemed like the Bears might be in trouble.

That's when Bronko Nagurski, one of the toughest players on the Bears, stepped up. He was known for running over defenders like a freight train, but this time, he made a key play with his arm.

Nagurski threw a pass to his teammate Bill Hewitt, who then quickly flipped the ball to Bill Karr. Karr caught it and sprinted 31 yards into the end zone for a touchdown!

"Go, Bill, go!" Halas shouted, running down the sideline as Karr sprinted toward the end zone.

The Bears were back in the lead, 23-21, and the crowd at Wrigley Field went wild. The game wasn't over yet, though.

The Giants still had a chance to score again, but the Bears' defense held strong. They stopped the Giants from getting any more points. When the game ended, the Chicago Bears were the first-ever NFL champions.

This victory was huge for the Bears. Not only did they win the very first championship game, but they also showed that they were one of the best teams in the league. George Halas, Bronko Nagurski, Red Grange, and the rest of the team became heroes in Chicago.

MONSTERS OF THE MIDWAY (1940)

In 1940, the Chicago Bears played one of the most legendary games in NFL history. This team was known as the "Monsters of the Midway." They were coached by the brilliant George Halas. He had a talent for finding the toughest, fastest, and smartest players. He had built a Bears team that was a true powerhouse. But this year, they were about to take it to a whole new level.

The Bears had a new trick up their sleeve. They had an offense called the T-Formation. In this formation, the quarterback would line up behind the center. The other players were arranged in a way that confused the other team.

It was nearly impossible for defenses to predict who would get the ball or which way the play was going. The Bears practiced this formation tirelessly, and it became their secret weapon.

That season, the Bears dominated their opponents, winning nine of their eleven games. They were a team full of superstars. Sid Luckman was a clever and strong-armed quarterback. Bill Osmanski was a quick and powerful running back.

The Bears faced the Washington Redskins at the NFL Championship Game on December 8, 1940. They were ready to show everyone just how powerful they were. But the game had a bit of extra drama, too. A few weeks earlier, the Redskins had actually defeated the Bears.

"Gentlemen," Halas began, his voice steady but intense, "three weeks ago, they called us 'crybabies.' Their coach said we quit when things got tough." He paused, letting the words sink in. "Today, we're going to teach them what Chicago football really means."

Halas and his players weren't about to forget that insult. They showed up to the game with a mission to prove the Redskins wrong.

The championship game was held in Washington, D.C., with over 36,000 fans packed into Griffith Stadium. No one could have predicted what was about to happen.

Right from the start, the Bears were unstoppable. On the Bears' second possession, Bill Osmanski lined up behind Luckman in the T-Formation.

"Red right, 98 cross!" Luckman barked. The ball was snapped, and magic unfolded.

Osmanski took the handoff, found a hole, and burst through the line. He dashed down the field, and scored a 68-yard touchdown! After that, it was like a snowball rolling down a hill. The Bears just kept piling on points. Their defense was equally ferocious, shutting down Washington's offense at every turn.

Sid Luckman led the Bears' offense brilliantly. He mixed up passes, handoffs, and used the T-Formation. It was so effectively that the Redskins' defense didn't know which way to turn.

Meanwhile, the Bears' defense didn't let Washington gain any ground. They tackled hard, hit even harder, and stopped the Redskins at every chance.

By halftime, the Bears were up 28-0, and the crowd was stunned. But the Bears weren't done yet. They came back in the second half and kept scoring. They didn't let up for a single play. It was like they were playing with all the energy they'd ever had, and they kept the pressure on until the very end.

When the game was finally over, the Bears had defeated the Redskins by an astonishing score of 73-0!

It was, and still is, the largest margin of victory in an NFL game, especially a championship game. They scored eleven touchdowns that day, with contributions from nearly every player on the team.

Afterward, the Bears celebrated a victory that fans would remember forever. The "T-Formation" they used became a guide for future teams. The 1940 Bears became a true legend in NFL history.

GALE SAYERS' SIX-TOUCHDOWN GAME (1965)

A thick fog rolled into Chicago on the afternoon of Friday, December 10, 1965, covering the city in a gray blanket. By Saturday night, the clouds finally broke open, and several inches of rain poured down. It set the stage for a muddy showdown between the Chicago Bears and the San Francisco 49ers on Sunday at Wrigley Field.

That cold, rainy day turned the field into a messy swamp. But on that muddy field, one of the greatest performances in Bears' history was about to occur.

Gale Sayers was a rookie who joined the Bears thirteen months ago. He had earned the nickname "Kansas Comet" for his incredible speed, agility, and ability to break tackles. But no one could have guessed just how amazing he'd be when he took the field against the 49ers.

As the teams took the field, the 49ers' defensive coordinator gathered his unit.

"Stay on your feet," he instructed. "This kid Sayers is quick, but nobody can run in this mud."

He would soon eat those words.

Sayers got things started with a bang. Early in the first quarter, quarterback Rudy Bukich threw a short pass to Sayers at the Chicago 20-yard line. Sayers caught it and was immediately swarmed by a group of 49ers.

"Got him!" a 49ers defender shouted.

But they didn't. Sayers took off as the San Francisco defenders struggled to keep their balance in the mud. He raced down the sideline for an 80-yard touchdown. The crowd erupted, and this was just the beginning.

The 49ers didn't know what to do. The weather was worse than any coach or player on the opposing sideline had expected. The conditions were impacting 21 of the 22 players on the field. The only one who didn't seem to mind was wearing No. 40 in navy and white.

Sayers performed another Houdini act in the second quarter. He took a handoff from Bukich at the San Francisco 21-yard line. He hurdled over one defender and swerved around two others. He powered through one more for another breathtaking score. A few minutes later, he tacked on his third touchdown of the game, a 7-yard run.

The fans could feel that they were witnessing something historic. His movements were so fast and sharp that defenders could barely touch him.

The score at halftime: 27-13, Chicago. The 49ers had no answer for the rookie running back. And with 30 minutes still to play, the Bears - and Sayers - were far from done.

In the third quarter, Sayers had one of those runs where nobody on the field could believe what happened. Sayers took the handoff and sprinted down the sideline. He left the 49ers defenders in his wake. With incredible speed and agility, he weaved around would-be tacklers. He charged his way to a 50-yard touchdown. It was his fourth touchdown of the day, and he made it look easy.

"No way he does it again," a 49ers coach said.

But he did. Sayers was given the ball close to the end zone for his fifth score. He powered through the line and crossed the goal line for a 1-yard touchdown. The score put the Bears up 40-13.

Just when everyone thought he couldn't possibly do more, Sayers lined up to return a punt. As the ball sailed through the air, the crowd held its breath. When Sayers caught it at the Chicago 15, he immediately made his move. He dodged a few defenders, and then he was off! With players from both teams slipping on the mud, he raced down the field for his sixth touchdown.

By the time the game ended, Gale Sayers had scored six touchdowns. He had tied the NFL record for most touchdowns in a single game.

The Bears went on to win the game 61-20, and Sayers finished with 336 all-purpose yards. That game didn't just make Sayers a legend in Chicago. It made him a legend in the entire NFL.

BEARS VS. COMMANDERS (WEEK 5, 2023)

The Chicago Bears were going through a rough time. They hadn't won a game in almost a whole year, and their fans were losing hope. But on a cool October night in 2023, the Bears were about to face the Washington Commanders on Thursday Night Football. With the whole country watching, they had one mission: end their losing streak and finally win a game.

Right from the start, things felt different. The Bears' quarterback, Justin Fields, came onto the field with a determined look. His star receiver, DJ Moore, was ready to make big plays.

The Bears' coach had spent all week planning special plays. He wanted to make sure Fields and Moore could connect like never before. And that plan worked perfectly.

In the pre-game warmups, Fields stood near midfield. He was watching Moore run routes.

"Hey DJ," Fields called out, a glint in his eye. "You feeling it tonight?"

Moore flashed his signature smile. "They ain't ready for what we're about to do."

As the teams lined up for the first quarter, the Bears' sideline buzzed with anticipation. Fields stepped into the huddle, looking each teammate in the eye.

"First play's for you, DJ," he said. "Let's show them what we've been working on."

The snap came, and Fields dropped back, his eyes locked downfield. He launched a deep pass down the sideline to Moore.

"GO GET IT, DJ!" Fields shouted as he watched his throw sail.

Moore didn't disappoint. He accelerated past the last defender, snatched the ball out of the air, and raced into the end zone.

Touchdown! The Bears' fans in the stadium roared, and you could feel the excitement building. It was just the beginning.

The Commanders tried to fight back, but the Bears' defense stepped up, too. They pressured Washington's quarterback, Sam Howell, and tackled hard. Every time Howell tried to get his team moving, Bears defenders were right there to stop him.

Fields and Moore weren't done yet. In the second quarter, Fields found Moore open once again. Moore took off, dodging defenders and speeding down the field for another touchdown.

The Commanders just couldn't stop the Bears' new star duo. By the end of the game, Fields had thrown four touchdown passes, and three of them were caught by DJ Moore. Moore ended up with an amazing 230 yards!

When the final whistle blew, the scoreboard read Bears 40, Commanders 20. The Bears had done it. They finally broke their 14-game losing streak.

The whole team celebrated on the field, hugging and high-fiving each other. Fields and Moore looked especially happy. They knew they'd played one of the best games of their careers.

CHAPTER FIVE QUIZ

1. What was the final score of the 1986 Super Bowl XX?

a. Bears 39, Patriots 30

b. Bears 35, Patriots 27

c. Bears 46, Patriots 10

d. Bears 49, Patriots 41

2. Who won the 1986 Super Bowl MVP?

a. Richard Dent

b. Jim McMahon

c. Walter Payton

d. Mike Singletary

3. Which year did the Chicago Bears win their first NFL Championship?

a. 1930

b. 1931

c. 1032

d. 1933

4. Which player scored the winning touchdown for the Chicago Bears in the first NFL Championship?

a. Bill Hewitt

b. Bill Karr

c. Bronko Nagurski

d. Carl Brumbaugh

5. Which team did the Bears defeat 73-0 in the 1940 NFL Championship Game?

a. San Francisco 49ers

b. Washington Redskins

c. Minnesota Vikings

d. Buffalo Bills

6. How many touchdowns did Gale Sayers score against the San Francisco 49ers on December 12, 1965?

a. 2

b. 3

c. 5

d. 6

7. Which team did the Chicago Bears defeat in 2023 to end a 14-game losing streak?

a. Washington Commanders

b. New York Giants

c. Dallas Cowboys

d. Green Bay Packers

Quiz Answers

1. Bears 46, Patriots 10 **2.** Richard Dent **3.** 1933 **4.** Bill Karr **5.** Washington Redskins **6.** 6 touchdowns **7.** Washington Commanders

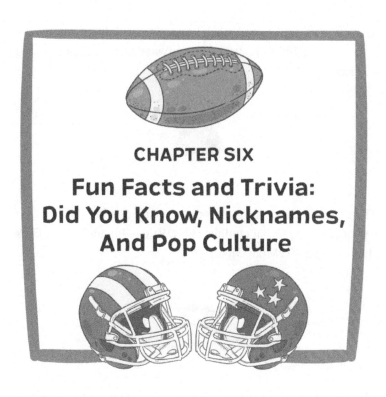

CHAPTER SIX

Fun Facts and Trivia: Did You Know, Nicknames, And Pop Culture

The team's mascot is Staley Da Bear, a super fun and energetic bear. He first showed up during the 2003 Chicago Bears season to make fans smile and have a great time at Soldier Field. Fans love cheering for him because he's always up to something wild and fun.

The Chicago Bears have retired the jersey numbers of fourteen legendary players, including 34 (Walter Payton), 51 (Dick Butkus), and 89 (Mike Ditka).

The nickname "Monsters of the Midway" didn't always belong to the Bears. It originally referred to a college football team in the 1930s. It was the University of Chicago Maroons.

The "Midway" in their nickname was named after a park on their campus called the Midway Plaisance. The university got rid of its football program in 1939. Later on, the Bears took over the famous nickname the following year.

The Bears have the most players in the Pro Football Hall of Fame. Some of the most recent Bears to be honored are Jimbo Covert, who was inducted in 2020, and Devin Hester, who was added in 2024.

The 1940 Chicago Bears team set the record for the biggest win in NFL history. They beat the Washington Redskins (now the Washington Commanders) 73-0 in the 1940 NFL Championship Game.

The Bears' fight song is called "Bear Down, Chicago Bears." It was written way back in 1941 by a famous songwriter named Al Hoffman. At home games, a version of the song recorded in

1993 by Bill Archer and the Big Bear Band, is played every time the Bears score. Fans love to hear it and sing along!

The Bears have signed a lot of amazing players, but their first big star was Harold "Red" Grange. He was a three-time All-American and a superstar running back for the University of Illinois.

Grange did something no one else has ever done. After his last college game on November 21, 1925, he joined the Bears just five days later! Because of this, the NFL made a new rule called the "Red Grange Rule," which stopped players from playing both college and pro football in the same season.

Caleb Williams was picked first overall by the Chicago Bears in the 2024 NFL draft. He became the first quarterback since 2002 to win his NFL debut after being picked first overall. Plus, he's the first Bears rookie quarterback to throw for 300 yards without any interceptions in a single game.

Mitchell Trubisky is the quickest Bears quarterback to reach 10,000 career passing yards, doing it in just 49 games! He was picked by the Chicago Bears in the first round, second overall, in the 2017 NFL draft. Trubisky played four seasons with the team.

Bronislau "Bronko" Nagurski was the first Bears player to run for 100 yards in a game. He rushed for 124 yards against the Portsmouth Spartans on November 26, 1933. Nagurski was a tough fullback and also played as a defensive tackle during his eight seasons with the Bears.

The all-time leading scorer for the Bears is Robbie Gould. He was their kicker from 2005 to 2015 and scored a total of 1,207 points.

Jay Cutler is the all-time passing leader for the Bears. He was their quarterback from 2009 to 2016 and threw for a total of 23,443 yards during his time with the team.

Gary Fencik is the all-time leader in interceptions and total tackles for the Bears. He was their safety from 1976 to 1987. He finished his career with 38 interceptions.

HERE ARE MORE QUESTIONS TO TEST YOUR KNOWLEDGE OF THE CHICAGO BEARS!

1. What are the official team colors of the Chicago Bears?

a. Navy Blue, Orange, and White

b. Green, Orange, and Silver

c. Pink, Navy Blue, and White

d. Purple, White, and Black

2. Who was the Bears' head coach before Matt Eberflus?

a. John Fox

b. Matt Nagy

c. Marc Trestman

d. Lovie Smith

3. Who was the first Bear to win the NFL Defensive Player of the Year award?

a. Mike Singletary

b. Richard Dent

c. Otis Wilson

d. Gale Sayers

4. Who holds the Bears' record for the most touchdown receptions in a season?

a. Ken Kavanaugh

b. Dick Gordon

c. Curtis Conway

d. Brandon Marshall

5. What is the nickname for the Bears' defensive line in the 1940s and 1980s?

a. Legion of Boom

b. Monsters of the Midway

c. Steel Curtain

d. Gang Green

6. In which season did the Bears add the letters "GSH" to the left sleeve of their jerseys to honor George Halas after he passed away?

a. 1980

b. 1982

c. 1984

d. 1987

7. Which kicker holds the record for the longest field goal in Chicago Bears history (58-yard)?

a. Robbie Gould

b. Cairo Santos

c. Kevin Butler

d. George Blanda

8. Who was the Bears' leading receiver in the 2023 season?

a. DJ Moore

b. Cole Kmet

c. Darnell Mooney

d. Allen Robinson

9. Which team did the Bears lose to in Super Bowl XLI on February 4, 2007?

a. Oakland Raiders

b. Indianapolis Colts

c. New England Patriots

d. Miami Dolphins

10. What was the Bears' original jersey color in the 1920s when they were called the Decatur Staleys?

a. Red

b. Light blue

c. Yellow

d. Black

11. Which 1980s Bears player had the nickname "The Refrigerator"?

a. Jim McMahon

b. William Perry

c. Richard Dent

d. Mike Ditka

12. In which year did the Bears first wear an all-white uniform in a game against the Detroit Lions?

a. 1948

b. 1967

c. 1995

d. 2024

13. Which team did the Bears face in their first game of the 2024 season?

a. Tennessee Titans

b. Green Bay Packers

c. Atlanta Falcons

d. New Orleans Saints

ABOUT THE AUTHOR

John Stevenson is a Michigan-based author of children's sports books. He is the father of two children, James and Tracy. When not writing new books, John can be found playing sports with his family or going on road trips. Through his books, John hopes to empower young readers and spark their imagination.

ENJOYED THE BOOK?

I'd really appreciate it if you could leave a review on Amazon. The number of reviews a book receives helps more people discover it. Even a short review can make a big difference, allowing me to keep doing what I love. Thank you in advance!

Trivia Answers

1. Navy Blue, Orange, and White **2.** Matt Nagy **3.** Mike Singletary **4.** Dick Gordon **5.** Monsters of the Midway **6.** 1984 **7.** Robbie Gould **8.** DJ Moore **9.** Indianapolis Colts **10.** Red **11.** William Perry **12.** 1995 **13.** Tennessee Titans

Made in the USA
Monee, IL
18 December 2024

74115999R00059